P-68.org

The Little Book

Second Edition

A Note

P-68.org: The Little Book is intended to be available free from on-line resources. E-book versions or printed versions may also be available or may become available. Where there is a charge for these e-book or printed versions, that charge should cover only the cost of creating, printing, and/or hosting those versions. No royalty payments or other payments of any description are made to the writers of this booklet.

Contents

Introduction

P-68.org is a 12-Step program for sex and relationship addicts.

This is what we do to recover in P-68.

1. We attend P-68 meetings. Most of us find that P-68 meetings are *vital.* We may attend other 12-step programs, but we have discovered that P-68 meetings seem to be the only place that we can learn how to recover from sex and relationship addiction.

2. We work the first nine Steps of the AA program as quickly as possible, even if we are not members of AA – even if we are not alcoholic.

3. We work Step 10 as a constant practice, even if we've not yet reached the Tenth Step in our Program. We also do Steps 11 and 12 as a daily practice, but we do Step 10 first, and we do it often.

4. We define and follow an abstinence list.

5. We go into withdrawal as soon as we can.

We describe elsewhere how we do these things.

This is a *suggested* program of recovery. Those P-68 members who do all these things seem to recover. But you are welcome to attend P-68 meetings, even if you're not yet ready to do these things yourself.

Suggested Meeting Format

1. Preamble
P-68 is a 12-Step program for sex and relationship addicts. If you think you might have problems with sex and/or relationships, you are welcome.

The P-68 program is based closely on the AA program of recovery, both the 12 Steps and 12 Traditions. We use the Big Book to guide our recovery, particularly the seven paragraphs on sex and relationships beginning at the bottom of page 68. We also follow closely its treatment of Steps 10 and 11 on pages 84-88.

In meetings, we discuss *solutions* to our sex and relationship problems, not the *details* of those problems. We suggest that you discuss such details outside the meeting with another member.

2. Moment of silence
Let's have *one minute of silence to quiet our minds*, followed by the Serenity Prayer.

3. Practice of Steps 10 and 11
Now we'll do Step 10, just as it suggests in the AA Big Book on page 84.

The Big Book says, *Continue to watch for selfishness, dishonesty, resentment, and fear.* Let's close or half-close our eyes. Now we ask ourselves:

Right here, right now, am I being selfish?

(Wait about ten seconds or so.)

Right here, right now, am I being dishonest?

(Wait about ten seconds or so.)

Right here, right now, am I resentful?

(Wait about ten seconds or so.)

Right here, right now, am I afraid?

(Wait about ten seconds or so.)

Now we ask ourselves:

Looking back over the last days or weeks, was I selfish, and some of that selfishness is still with me?

(Wait about ten seconds or so.)

Looking back over the last days or weeks, was I dishonest, and some of that dishonesty is still with me?

(Wait about ten seconds or so.)

Looking back over the last days or weeks, was I resentful, and some of that resentment is still with me?

(Wait about ten seconds or so.)

Looking back over the last days or weeks, was I afraid, and some of that fear is still with me?

(Wait about ten seconds or so.)

Now the Big Book says, *When these crop up, we ask God at once to remove them.* Let's close or half-close our eyes, and ask whatever Higher Power we have to remove the selfishness, dishonesty, resentment, or fear. When you've done that, open your eyes.

Now the Big Book says, *We discuss them with someone immediately.* We tell someone how we are feeling. Remember, the focus is on the *feeling.* Don't spend too much time on the details of *why* you feel the way you feel. In groups of twos or threes, let's do this part of the Step.

(Give three or four minutes for the discussion.)

Now the Big Book says, *We make amends quickly if we have harmed anyone.* Let's close or half-close our eyes. Let's ask ourselves, *Do I owe an amend around what I just discussed?* The answer may be *yes* or *no.* When you know the answer, open your eyes.

Now the Big Book says, *Then we resolutely turn our thoughts to someone we can help.* Let's close or half-close our eyes, and think of someone we can help. When you've thought of someone, open your eyes.

Now the Big Book says, *Love and tolerance of others is our code.* Let's close or half-close our eyes. We ask ourselves, *Do I now feel love, or at least a little more tolerance, for the people I thought about during this session?* When you know the answer, open your eyes.

At the bottom of page 87, at the start of the last paragraph, there is a brief summary of Step 11. It says, *As we go through the day, we pause when agitated or doubtful and ask for the right thought or action.*

Let's close, or half-close our eyes. We ask ourselves, *Right here, right now, am I agitated? Right here, right now, am I doubtful?* Because we have just done Step 10, **we may be uncertain.** We may not know what to do about the issues that we discussed.

The Big Book says on page 69, *In meditation, we ask God what we should do.* Using that suggestion, let's take four minutes to ask our Higher Power for the right thought or action. You may wish to meditate, to pray, or just to sit in silence.

4. Continue with the discussion part of the meeting

(You can:

- *Ask for a topic, or come up with a topic yourself;*
- *Read one or more paragraphs from page 12, paragraph 5 of this book and ask people to comment from their experience.*

Pass the basket at some point during the meeting.)

5. At the end of the meeting

All P-68 written information can be found at http://www.p-68.org. You can also buy a printed copy of *P-68: The Little Book* on-line at cost by going to https://www.createspace.com/5092610

Are there any P-68 announcements?

Now let us close the meeting with *(choose a way to close the meeting).*

P-68 Basics

1. What is P-68?
P-68 is a 12-Step fellowship focusing on recovery from sex and relationship addiction. We use the Twelve Steps and Twelve Traditions of Alcoholics Anonymous. In fact, our approach to recovery from sex and relationship addiction is based mainly on the text of *Alcoholics Anonymous* – the Big Book.

2. Why does P-68 rely so heavily on the text of the AA Big Book?
Sex and sex-based relationships are the only addiction other than alcoholism which receives extended attention in the Big Book. Even though it is intended for recovering alcoholics, the Big Book addresses seven paragraphs to sexual matters in its treatment of Step 4 (the inventory Step). It is our experience that sex and relationship addicts who study and apply those seven paragraphs will recover from their addiction. We will need to do some other things as well, but putting those seven paragraphs into practice seems to be essential.

3. What other things do recovering sex and relationship addicts need?
We need:

a. *Attendance at P-68 meetings.* This is presently a problem, as there are few or no P-68 meetings. If it is not possible to attend P-68 meetings, we may choose to attend SLAA, SAA, or similar meetings;

b. *The Twelve Steps.* Recovering sex and relationship addicts are encouraged to work the first nine of these as quickly as possible. There is no reason for the first nine Steps to take more than a month or two at the outside;

c. *A constant, moment-by-moment practice of Step 10 from the very beginning of our recovery* – in other words, long before we reach Step 10 as we work through the Steps. We say more about the working of Step 10 below;

d. *An abstinence list.* The abstinence list is a list of behaviors which we believe we can abstain from for some specific period of time *with the help of our Higher Power.* We say more about the abstinence list below;

e. *A period (possibly more than one period) of withdrawal.* At the start of our recovery, we deliberately choose to withdraw from most or all of our present sexual and relationship-based activities. We do this for an indefinite period of time. We say more about withdrawal below;

f. *And finally ... Desperation.* In our experience, P-68 works well for sex and relationship addicts who are, for one reason or another, desperate. P-68 seems to be of little use to people who are having mild problems with sex and relationships, or who are looking for a self-help group.

4. What is the difference between P-68 and other 12-Step fellowships that focus on addictions around sex and relationships?
The main difference is P-68's use of the AA Big Book, in particular the seven paragraphs beginning at the bottom of p. 68 and the treatment of the practice of Step 10 in the middle of p. 84.

Other 12-Step fellowships have their own literature, their own "Big Books," sometimes their own versions of the Twelve Steps and Twelve Traditions: P-68 does not. We focus very strongly on withdrawal and the abstinence list, though our approach to the abstinence list is unusual. Otherwise, P-68 is a Big Book-focused fellowship.

5. What are the seven paragraphs from the AA Big Book that talk about sex and relationships?
Here they are:

> *Now about sex. Many of us needed an overhauling there. But above all, we tried to be sensible on this question. It's so easy to get way off the track. Here we find human opinions running to extremes—absurd extremes, perhaps. One set of voices cry that sex is a lust of our lower nature, a base necessity of procreation. Then we have the voices who cry for sex and more sex; who bewail the institution of marriage; who think that most of the troubles of the race are traceable to sex causes. They think we*

do not have enough of it, or that it isn't the right kind. They see its significance everywhere. One school would allow man no flavor for his fare and the other would have us all on a straight pepper diet. We want to stay out of this controversy. We do not want to be the arbiter of anyone's sex conduct. We all have sex problems. We'd hardly be human if we didn't. What can we do about them?

We reviewed our own conduct over the years past. Where had we been selfish, dishonest, or inconsiderate? Whom had we hurt? Did we unjustifiably arouse jealousy, suspicion or bitterness? Where were we at fault, what should we have done instead? We got this all down on paper and looked at it.

In this way we tried to shape a sane and sound ideal for our future sex life. We subjected each relation to this test—was it selfish or not? We asked God to mold our ideals and help us to live up to them. We remembered always that our sex powers were God-given and therefore good, neither to be used lightly or selfishly nor to be despised and loathed.

Whatever our ideal turns out to be, we must be willing to grow toward it. We must be willing to make amends where we have done harm, provided that we do not bring about still more harm in so doing. In other words, we treat sex as we would any other problem. In meditation, we ask God what we should do about each specific matter. The right answer will come, if we want it.

God alone can judge our sex situation. Counsel with persons is often desirable, but we let God be the final judge. We realize that some people are as fanatical about sex as others are loose. We avoid hysterical thinking or advice.

Suppose we fall short of the chosen ideal and stumble? Does this mean we are going to get drunk? Some people tell us so. But this is only a half-truth. It depends on us and on our motives. If we are sorry for what we have done, and have the honest desire to let God take us to better things, we believe we will be forgiven and will have learned our lesson. If we are not sorry, and our conduct continues to harm others, we are quite sure to drink. We are not theorizing. These are facts out of our experience.

To sum up about sex: We earnestly pray for the right ideal, for guidance in each questionable situation, for sanity, and for the strength to do the right thing. If sex is very troublesome, we throw ourselves the harder into helping others. We think of their needs and work for them. This takes us out of ourselves. It quiets the imperious urge, when to yield would mean heartache.

6. What is the abstinence list?

The abstinence list is a list of behaviors and actions which recovering sex and relationship addicts make up. We list behaviors and actions which have caused us problems in the past, and which we believe we can abstain from *with the help of our Higher Power* for a finite period of time.

7. What does an abstinence list look like?

It consists of a series of actions or behaviors from which we will abstain with the help of our Higher Power; the corrective measures we take if we find ourselves performing the action or the behavior; and a time period during which we will abstain.

It is important to note that there is a specific period of time assigned to each behavior or action. For example, we say that we will abstain from the behavior or action for a week, or for two weeks, or for a month.

It is also important to understand that we commit to abstain from each behavior or action *with the help of our Higher Power.* We are not going to be able to do it on the basis of will power, nor are we making a commitment to anyone else in Program such as a sponsor. We are making the commitment to, and with the help of, our Higher Power.

Sample statements might be:

- I will not masturbate for a week (or whatever period of time);
- For the next month, if I find I am staring at a woman/man, I will turn away the moment I realize it and, if I need to do so, I will call someone in Program and talk to them about it;

- For the next two weeks, if I find myself fantasizing about Person X, I will ask my Higher Power to help take that obsession away, and I will silently say the Serenity Prayer;
- I will not be alone with just one woman/man for the next two weeks.

8. Can the addict change the list?

Yes, at any time … provided we tell our sponsor *before* making the change. Even though we have committed to the behavior or action for a specific duration, we may change our mind at any time *provided we call our sponsor first and tell him or her.* As long as we tell our sponsor about the change in our abstinence list, we may then indulge in the behavior … *and we are still abstinent, because we are following our (now modified) abstinence list.*

9. That seems as though it is open to all kinds of abuse.

Yes, it does. It seems to say that we can commit to abstain from a behavior and then, the moment we feel like doing it, we can call our sponsor, take the item off the list, do it, and then call our sponsor back and put the item on the list again.

It certainly looks as though that would happen, but our experience suggests otherwise. Remember that we *must call our sponsor before changing our abstinence list.* Typically, therefore, we may call and put something on the abstinence list, then call again and take it off, call again and put it on again, and call again and take it off … and then one of two things usually happens. Either we leave it on the abstinence list, and get on with the rest of our program, or else we quit the fellowship altogether. In fact, if we are "chopping and changing" in this way, our sponsor may *suggest* that we try and "recover" by ourselves for a while. You will remember that we cited *desperation* as one of the things needed to recover in P-68. Addicts, or potential addicts, who are not desperate enough to persist with the abstinence list probably need to go back out and create some more pain for themselves.

10. Why do addicts come up with the abstinence list themselves? Wouldn't it be much more effective if a sponsor told them what to put on the abstinence list?

Our experience suggests that this will not work. In the seven paragraphs from the AA Big Book quoted above, we find the following sentence: *We do not want to be the arbiter of anyone's sex conduct.* What should be on our abstinence list is between us and our Higher Power. It is no one's business but ours. Since we "do not want to be the arbiter of anyone's sex conduct," we do not tell other people in P-68 what should be on their abstinence lists, nor do we expect them to tell us what should be on ours.

So if we call our sponsor and say we want to modify our abstinence list in some way, it is not the sponsor's job either to encourage or to discourage the change – and for the same reason given in the previous paragraph. We do not need to worry about "making a mistake" with our abstinence list. If we do indeed "make a mistake," the resulting pain will drive us to correct it ... or to leave the P-68 fellowship altogether, which is something we may need to do if we are insufficiently desperate.

There is an informal tradition in many 12-Step fellowships that sponsors should have all the answers and should tell sponsees what to do. Our experience in P-68 suggests that this will not work when sponsoring sex and relationship addicts. An addict in P-68 who has a strongly directive sponsor will probably be better off finding another sponsor.

11. Will there come a time when the recovering addict no longer needs an abstinence list?
Yes, that is possible. But some of us with double-digit years of recovery still have such a list, or may start one from time to time.

12. What is withdrawal?
Withdrawal is a period of time, usually at the beginning of recovery, when we voluntarily withdraw from all or most sexual activity and all or most intimate relationships *for an indefinite period of time.*

We find it's best to create a special version of an abstinence list for withdrawal purposes. Generally speaking, our abstinence lists have a time period next to each behavior from which we want to abstain. But the withdrawal list is different. The actions and behaviors from which we are withdrawing will all appear on our withdrawal list, *but without a period of time next to any of those behaviors or actions.* This is because withdrawal is "open-ended": we do not know when we start it how long it will last.

The purpose of withdrawal is to experience, often for the first time, what ordinary life is like without the escapes of sexual activity or unhealthy intimate relationships. Because we addicts have used these things for many years to protect us against the things we fear most – loneliness, abandonment, and so on – the period of withdrawal is painful. *It is meant to be painful.* During this period, we will depend very strongly upon our practice of Step 10 to get us through.

Some of us commit to periods of withdrawal when we are well into our recovery. It can be a useful practice if we find we are getting sloppy about our abstinence.

13. Can the recovering sex and relationship addict skip withdrawal?
Our collective experience suggests that it cannot be avoided. Sooner or later, it has to be done … so it might just as well be sooner, because delaying it will only increase its painfulness.

14. How long should withdrawal last?
There is no fixed time. We each determine for ourselves when the period of withdrawal should come to an end. Typically, it lasts several months.

15. How painful is withdrawal, compared to (say) withdrawal from alcohol or drugs?
Our experience is that it is more painful emotionally. It is certainly much longer.

16. What is Step 10?
The Step itself reads: *Continued to take personal inventory, and when we were wrong promptly admitted it.* The practice of it is covered in half a paragraph on page 84 of the AA Big Book, and reads: *Continue to watch for selfishness, dishonesty, resentment, and fear. When these crop up, we ask God at once to remove them. We discuss them with someone immediately, and make amends quickly if we have harmed anyone. Then we resolutely turn our thoughts to someone we can help. Love and tolerance of others is our code.*

17. Why is the practice of Step 10 from the very start of recovery so important?
Because the practice of Step 10 makes us watch – in particular, it makes us watch ourselves, our thoughts and our feelings. All the trouble, pain, and suffering we have caused ourselves and others occurred because, instead of *watching* our thoughts and feelings, we merely *listened* to them and then did what our thoughts and feelings told us to do. If we do not know what we are thinking and feeling, if we do not watch our thoughts and feelings, then we will inevitably be driven by them.

18. So watching our thoughts and feelings enables us to control them?
No. We *never* reach the point where we can control our thoughts and feelings. Watching is simply the first step in dealing with them as they arise.

19. So when we feel bad, we tell someone else about it?
Not just yet. The first thing we do is to ask God as we understand God to take away any selfishness, dishonesty, resentment, or fear. Then – if we need to – we talk to someone about them.

20. And does this process make the thoughts and feelings go away?
The thoughts and feelings are not the problem, although because we are addicts we *think* that they are a problem. And doing Step 10 will not necessarily make them go away, though over a period of time we find that our thoughts and feelings become less troublesome.

21. So if this process doesn't necessarily make them go away, why do Step 10?
Because we know of no other method which will teach us how to feel and think without acting on those thoughts and feelings. It may take some time for Step 10 to work, even if we do it over and over; but eventually it *will* work. And nothing else we have tried *does* work.

22. When will the recovering sex and relationship addict be able to have an intimate, possibly physical, relationship with another person?
This may seem very strange, but the purpose of the P-68 program is not to prepare us for intimate or sexual relationships. To focus on re-

engaging in these relationships is to continue to live in the obsession with sex and relationships. And the whole reason for starting recovery in the first place is to be rid, as far as possible, of that obsession.

At some point during our recovery, we start to become aware of the advantages of being alone. (If, on the other hand, our addiction has manifested itself in being constantly alone – what is called *anorexia* – we may instead become aware of the advantages of being in a relationship.) Sometimes we actively like being alone, or perhaps with casual friends in whom we have no physical interest. Eventually we will reach the point where we see that *there are just as many advantages, and just as many disadvantages, to being alone as there are to being in a relationship.* At that point, we may be ready to explore the possibility of such a relationship.

23. How do we learn how to do this? Do we have a dating plan? Who gives us advice on what to do?
Once more, to ask questions like these is to remain in the obsession with sex and relationships. If our Higher Power is able to direct us towards recovery, we can be quite sure that our Higher Power will be able to guide us if and when we feel we are being drawn to engage in intimate relationships again.

Because we work the first nine Steps of Program quickly, we are then free to live our lives based on the last three Steps. The practice of Steps 10 and 11 is covered in pages 84-88 of the Big Book, and we use those pages, together with our practice of Step 12, to deal with all matters that arise in our lives, including the matter of re-engaging in intimate relationships.

24. I have read what you have suggested and I'm sorry, but I'm not prepared to do it.
That's OK. Don't do it.

If you are a sex and relationship addict, you may find what you need in other fellowships. We didn't find what we needed there, but that doesn't mean that you won't.

Or perhaps you are not an addict after all; or perhaps you can solve your problem with therapy, or with self-help books or groups, or by going to church.

If there is any doubt in your mind as to whether you need the P-68 program, we strongly encourage you to try *all* possible alternatives. If you try all those other alternatives and they don't work, then you will get desperate, and what we have to offer seems to work best for truly desperate sex and relationship addicts.

Sponsors and Sponsees

Sponsorship in P-68 is different from sponsorship in many other 12-Step programs. Let's see how – and why – P-68 sponsorship is distinctive.

The basics of recovery
Recovery in P-68 is based on:
- Attendance at meetings
- The Twelve Steps
- A constant practice of Step 10
- An abstinence list
- A period of withdrawal
- Desperation

If you have an abstinence list; if you have been through a period of withdrawal; if you practice Step 10 constantly; if you have worked the first nine Steps and now live in the last three; if you attend meetings regularly; and if you understand that only complete desperation can ever drive a sex and relationship addict to practice these things himself – then you may be ready to sponsor another member of P-68.

Not-knowing
In many other 12-Step programs, sponsors tend to be regarded as experts or gurus and are often supposed to have all the answers for the newcomer.

In P-68, the situation is pretty much the opposite. As a sponsor, the most beneficial thing you can share with sponsees is your ignorance of what they should do. As long as your sponsees are following the basics of recovery, as listed above, *we believe that you do not know any better than them what they should do. And we believe that you should tell them so.*

Recovery in P-68 is based on the text of the AA Big Book, and particularly on the seven paragraphs on sex beginning at the bottom of p. 68. There you will find the phrase:

We do not want to be the arbiter of anyone's sex conduct.

In other words, it is not our job as sponsors to tell our sponsees what should or should not be on their abstinence lists, or what their withdrawal should consist of.

What P-68 sponsors do

P-68 sponsors:

- share their experience, strength, and hope – not their opinion or advice
- listen to what behaviors and actions their sponsees wish to put on their abstinence list
- listen to and accept any changes that sponsees may wish to make to the abstinence list
- are the "go-to" people when their sponsees are doing Step 10 and need someone to listen to their thoughts and feelings
- take sponsees *quickly* through the first nine Steps, always remembering that their sponsees' recovery will be on God's time, not the sponsors'
- attend meetings with their sponsees
- show their sponsees *exactly* how to practice Step 10 on an ongoing basis
- encourage the ongoing practice of the last three Steps when the first nine are completed
- remember that having sponsees "go back out" may be a far better way of convincing them to work this program than trying to tell them, or persuade them of, what they should do

What P-68 sponsor *do not* do

P-68 sponsors do not:

- tell their sponsees what behaviors and actions should be on their abstinence list

- try and dissuade sponsees from making changes to the abstinence list, or make recommendations as to what changes should be made
- tell sponsees what to do when they talk about their Step 10

P-68 sponsors' personal ignorance of what their sponsees should do is one of the greatest gifts they can give to those they are sponsoring

A Commentary on the Page 68 Paragraphs in Alcoholics Anonymous (The Big Book)

The Seven Paragraphs From The AA Big Book on Sex and Relationships

Now about sex. Many of us needed an overhauling there. But above all, we tried to be sensible on this question. It's so easy to get way off the track. Here we find human opinions running to extremes—absurd extremes, perhaps. One set of voices cry that sex is a lust of our lower nature, a base necessity of procreation. Then we have the voices who cry for sex and more sex; who bewail the institution of marriage; who think that most of the troubles of the race are traceable to sex causes. They think we do not have enough of it, or that it isn't the right kind. They see its significance everywhere. One school would allow man no flavor for his fare and the other would have us all on a straight pepper diet. We want to stay out of this controversy. We do not want to be the arbiter of anyone's sex conduct. We all have sex problems. We'd hardly be human if we didn't. What can we do about them?

We reviewed our own conduct over the years past. Where had we been selfish, dishonest, or inconsiderate? Whom had we hurt? Did we unjustifiably arouse jealousy, suspicion or bitterness? Where were we at fault, what should we have done instead? We got this all down on paper and looked at it.

In this way we tried to shape a sane and sound ideal for our future sex life. We subjected each relation to this test—was it selfish or not? We asked God to mold our ideals and help us to live up to them. We remembered always that our sex powers were God-given and therefore good, neither to be used lightly or selfishly nor to be despised and loathed.

Whatever our ideal turns out to be, we must be willing to grow toward it. We must be willing to make amends where we have done harm, provided that we do not bring about still more harm in so doing. In other words, we treat sex as we would any other problem. In meditation, we ask God what we should do about each specific matter. The right answer will come, if we want it.

God alone can judge our sex situation. Counsel with persons is often desirable, but we let God be the final judge. We realize that some people are as fanatical about sex as others are loose. We avoid hysterical thinking or advice.

Suppose we fall short of the chosen ideal and stumble? Does this mean we are going to get drunk? Some people tell us so. But this is only a half-truth. It depends on us and on our motives. If we are sorry for what we have done, and have the honest desire to let God take us to better things, we believe we will be forgiven and will have learned our lesson. If we are not sorry, and our conduct continues to harm others, we are quite sure to drink. We are not theorizing. These are facts out of our experience.

To sum up about sex: We earnestly pray for the right ideal, for guidance in each questionable situation, for sanity, and for the strength to do the right thing. If sex is very troublesome, we throw ourselves the harder into helping others. We think of their needs and work for them. This takes us out of ourselves. It quiets the imperious urge, when to yield would mean heartache.

The P-68 Commentary

Now about sex. Many of us needed an overhauling there.

This must be one of the great understatements in the Big Book of *Alcoholics Anonymous.* It has been estimated that about 50% of the men recovering in AA – men, that is, who have stopped drinking, sometimes for a considerable time – have enough problems with sex and relationships that they should be in a 12-Step program that deals with these matters. For younger men –

say, men younger than 30 years of age or so – the estimate is higher: perhaps 80% or more. The statistics may be similar for women. *Remember, these estimates are for supposedly **sober** alcoholics – not for practicing drinkers.*

Even though it was written as long ago as the 1930s, the Big Book suggests that this problem is so huge for recovering alcoholics that a third of their Step 4 inventory should be devoted to the subject. This is a remarkably large proportion, not least because *addiction to sex and relationships is the **only** addiction other than alcoholism about which the Big Book has anything to say.* In other words, a third of the recovering alcoholic's Step 4 will be devoted to a potential addiction other than alcoholism.

Because the writers of the Big Book focused this attention on an addiction other than alcoholism, and because nearly all recovering alcoholics have completed Step 4, we would expect that these seven paragraphs would be read with interest and followed to the letter by recovering alcoholics.

But the facts are the complete opposite. Many recovering alcoholics appear never to have read these paragraphs at all. Others may have read them, but they pay scant attention to them. The majority of recovering alcoholics certainly have no notion that these seven paragraphs offer a pattern for living a life that is relatively free of obsession with sex and relationships. As a result, problems with sex and relationships are a silent scourge in AA and other 12-Step programs. The terrible warnings about the results of *not* following the recommendations of these seven paragraphs – warnings we will be examining later – are all too frequently realized in Program. When someone goes "back out" and drinks or uses again, the chances are very good that sex and relationships are a large part of the reason.

If sex and relationship problems exist in AA, they are everywhere outside the walls of Program too. We live in a world where the conventions put in place by society over the centuries to help us handle sex and relationships have more or less disappeared. Religions in the west no longer act as a control on most people's behavior. An approach to sex and relationships based on secular (i.e. non-religious) morality or ethics has also failed us. The consequence is that sex and relationships, historically an area closely guided by religious or ethical authorities, has become a subject on which everyone decides for themselves what they will do. And what they do decide to do is at best making them unhappy. In some cases, it's getting them to the point of misery, desperation, and – if they are substance addicts – death.

Yes, most of us need an overhaul. In fact, most of us – in or out of Program – need more than an overhaul. We need a complete reconstruction in the area of sex and relationships. And since using our brains got us into this mess to begin with, we can be pretty sure that using those same brains is not going to get us out of it. It's going to take much, much more than that.

But above all, we tried to be sensible on this question. It's so easy to get way off the track. Here we find human opinions running to extremes—absurd extremes, perhaps. One set of voices cry that sex is a lust of our lower nature, a base necessity of procreation. Then we have the voices who cry for sex and more sex; who bewail the institution of marriage; who think that most of the troubles of the race are traceable to sex causes. They think we do not have enough of it, or that it isn't the right kind. They see its significance everywhere. One school would allow man no flavor for his fare and the other would have us all on a straight pepper diet.

It's hard to believe that this was written in the 1930s. What would the writers of the AA Big Book – Bill Wilson, and the members of the New York group – say if they were to return and see what a disaster we have made of this area … *including members of AA?*

What is interesting about this section is that it talks about *human opinion* – that is, about *what people in general say about sex.*

Now, the Big Book was written against a background of what people in general in the 1930s had to say about *alcoholism*. And what they had to say about alcoholism was ill-informed, inaccurate, and useless to the suffering alcoholic. Alcoholism was basically regarded as a moral weakness. (It isn't – it's an addiction.) Alcoholics were regarded as people who lacked will-power. (That, of course, is ridiculous: witness the countless successful attempts of alcoholics and addicts who use willpower to lay hands on their drug of choice wherever they may be and whatever time of day it is, regardless of difficulties.) It was thought that, if they were made to feel ashamed of their behavior, they might conceivably reform themselves. (Quite useless, of course, since addicts are experts on handling personal shame and guilt, usually with more alcohol and drugs.) It was thought that they must be suffering from a mental illness, and that psychiatrists or psychologists might be able to help. (This worked occasionally, but no more than occasionally.) It was hoped that some sort of medical breakthrough might be around the corner which could help. Even in the 1930s, that was regarded as pretty much of a long shot. (The Big Book says, "Physicians who are familiar with alcoholism agree there is no such thing as making a normal drinker out of an alcoholic. Science may one day accomplish this, but it hasn't done so yet." Many decades later, most people agree.)

In other words, the reason that people didn't seem to be able to do anything about the problem of alcoholism was that *most of them weren't alcoholics themselves.* They thought they knew what the alcoholic should do; but they weren't alcoholics, so they could not be of much help. AA succeeded because it was started by two men who had a particularly deep interest in finding a solution *to their own alcoholism.* When they found that solution, their story was compelling to other alcoholics precisely because – as alcoholics – the two founders knew exactly what they were talking about.

The reason that this is important – and it's easy to forget nowadays – is that previous attempts to control alcoholism had often centered around some form of temperance or prohibition –

in other words, a "solution" that would be imposed on everyone, whether they needed it or not. The Washingtonian movement of the nineteenth century *began* as a movement to help people with alcohol problems, but it died because it started to focus on other matters such as temperance or politics. The peculiar genius of AA is that *it has no interest in whether people in general have a problem with alcohol.* Instead, it says to each potential member, "Do *you* think *you* have a problem with alcohol?"

So much for alcohol and alcoholism. The section of the paragraph we are reading at this stage is making the same point about sex and relationships. It observes that the world has several, often extreme, opinions about sex. But – in just the same way that the view of non-alcoholics about alcoholism is often of little help to the suffering alcoholic – the views of the world about sex and relationships are going to be of little use to the suffering sex and relationship addict. Ordinary men and women can drink. Recovering alcoholics can't. Ordinary men and women may have extreme views about sex and relationships, and may manifest those views in extreme forms of behavior. But what is important for the sex and relationship addict is not learning to imitate what men and women in the "real world" may think and do. It's much more personal than that. What matters to suffering sex and relationship addicts is *how they can recover.* And to get the answer to that, they need to talk to other, *genuinely recovering* sex and relationship addicts – not to try and imitate what supposedly "normal" people may think, say, and do about sex and relationships.

There is another problem that this section points to: Most people who are sex and relationship addicts don't think it's a very big deal. Yes, they may get into sexual relationships too readily, and then the relationship goes wrong, there's a breakup, and they feel awful. Or they may sleep casually with someone, and feel bad about that afterwards. But there is always a cure, of course: another relationship. The great difference between substance addiction on the one hand, and sex and relationship addiction on the other, is that *by and large sex and relationship addicts think they're leading a normal life* – it's just that they suspect they're handling it badly, perhaps because they're with the wrong lover. In fact, as a society we not only recognize this behavior, *we think it's funny*. It's the stuff of sitcoms. It's hard to imagine a sitcom based on alcoholics or addicts getting drunk or high and then destroying themselves and everyone around them. But sex and relationship addiction is somehow amusing, somehow OK. In other words, most sex and relationship addicts don't think they have a real problem with sex and relationships. *And nor do the people by whom they're surrounded.* In fact, sometimes even other people in AA may think it's just fine, as long as the alcoholic doesn't drink over it. Some of us have had AA sponsors who said it was all right to act out sexually as long as we didn't drink. It's as though there were an outbreak of a potentially deadly disease in the world, but both the sufferers and the people around them thought that there was no real problem.

And that has caused some people in 12-Step programs for sex or relationship addiction to believe that *they can, and ought to, learn to be like "normal" people.* Perhaps they can; but we members of P-68 don't believe that *we* can. Instead, we learn to let our Higher Power handle the entire matter of sex and relationships *from start to finish.* We've given up on the idea that we can ever figure this out on our own or with assistance from friends or self-help books. *We surrender completely* to the idea that only our Higher Power can tell us what to do about sex and relationships, and give us the strength to carry it out. *This is why one of the foundations of P-68 is* **desperation.** Typically, we see that sex and relationship addicts who aren't desperate find it difficult to follow our way of life.

We want to stay out of this controversy. We do not want to be the arbiter of anyone's sex conduct. We all have sex problems. We'd hardly be human if we didn't. What can we do about them?

This paragraph contains one of the great guidelines for recovery from sex and relationship addiction: *We do not want to be the arbiter of anyone's sex conduct.* This principle is another of the foundations of P-68. Recovering sex and relationship addicts have to determine for themselves, with the help of their Higher Power, what their behavior should be; and then they have to depend on that Higher Power to help them carry that out. This is why we in P-68 regard sponsorship as so important, because of what P-68 sponsors are *not: They are not, and never will be, an expert on their sponsees' behavior with respect to sex and relationships.* They are merely a "witness" to the relationship between their sponsees and their sponsees' Higher Power.

We think this point is so important that it is worth making again. For us, it is not possible to recover from sex and relationship addiction based on what other members of P-68 think or say we should do. We must work this out ourselves with the help of our Higher Power. Recovery in P-68 does not come from imitating the behavior of other members, but from a direct relationship with a Higher Power – whatever we may consider that Higher Power to be – who will guide us in our sex conduct.

We reviewed our own conduct over the years past. Where had we been selfish, dishonest, or inconsiderate? Whom had we hurt? Did we unjustifiably arouse jealousy, suspicion or bitterness? Where were we at fault, what should we have done instead? We got this all down on paper and looked at it.

Now the Big Book tells us how we are to achieve the goal of establishing an ideal for sex and relationships. Remember that it has already been determined that we cannot do this on our own: we may have to do a great deal of personal work, but this is only a preparation for allowing our Higher Power to guide us.

The Big Book suggests that we write down a review of our previous conduct with regard to sex and relationships. This is not some lurid history of our sexual or "romantic" past. Instead, it is recommended that we ask specific questions about those old relationships. The predominant focus is on our *selfishness*, which the Big Book has already suggested lies at the heart of every problem we have ("Selfishness, self-centeredness! That, we think, is the root of our troubles" – page 62.) The questions we should answer about those relationships are listed clearly. Where, in each relationship, had we been selfish? Where, in each relationship, had we been dishonest? Where, in each relationship, had we been inconsiderate? Who were the people we had hurt? Where, without justification, did we arouse jealousy? Suspicion? Bitterness? Where we were at fault, what should we have done differently? Note that this analysis is about *us*, not about the other person. This is not a revisiting of the supposed faults of other people. This is about *us*, and the focus should be solely on ourselves. And all of this should be written down. Once it's written down, the Big Book suggests that *we look at it*. Like so much else in Step 4, this is not the recording of information that we are going to read aloud monotonously in our Step 5. (See *An Unpopular Guide to Step 5* for more on this topic.) We are writing these things down for a very specific and personal reason: we are attempting to develop an *ideal* for any future sex-based or intimate relationships. We then look carefully at what we have written because doing so will help us to establish that ideal.

In this way we tried to shape a sane and sound ideal for our future sex life. We subjected each relation to this test—was it selfish or not? We asked God to mold our ideals and help us to live up to them. We remembered always that our sex powers were God-given and therefore good, neither to be used lightly or selfishly nor to be despised and loathed.

We cannot emphasize enough that all this effort is expended in pursuit of an *ideal*. An ideal is something we work towards. It is not necessarily something we are going to achieve all the time, but it is a goal for which we strive.

This ideal is an ideal *for us*. We are not talking here about some ideal partner for a future relationship. Future relationships are none of our business: if and when they come, they will be the business of our Higher Power. So we are not talking about some other ideal person. We are talking about an ideal *for ourselves.*

This ideal is intended to replace the motives that drove us previously, nearly all of which arose out of *selfishness.* We had sex, or we entered a relationship, primarily because of what we could get out of it. We wanted sex, and so we lied to get it. We fell in love, and said or did whatever was necessary to get the other person to fall in love with us. We wanted to dominate another person because we got a rush out of it. We were prepared to demean ourselves as long as the other person didn't abandon us, because we were terrified of being alone. We bullied our partner to change, because how our partner looked and spoke and acted reflected poorly – so we believed – on us. As we look back over what we have written in our Step Four, we see that, in the main, we were driven fundamentally by selfishness in many of our sex- and relationship-based actions.

It's that selfishness which is to be replaced with an ideal. Notice that we are talking here about an ideal that is a *basis* for the way we will think and act in the future. It's an ideal for our own behavior. The selfishness that drove us in the past must progressively disappear, but as it disappears it has to be replaced with an ideal *which cannot come from us alone.* How can it? We are selfish, self-centered people. That ideal must be molded by our Higher Power. We know that we cannot continue to be driven by selfishness any longer, but as far as determining what should replace that selfishness, we are out of ideas. So we use Step 10 to see where we are being selfish, we admit to our Higher Power that we have no idea what to do about that selfishness other than asking our Higher Power to remove it, and then we use the rest of Steps 10 and 11 to have that Higher Power tell us what to do.

There is nothing "disgusting" or disgraceful about sex when the element of selfishness is removed. The Big Book is quite clear about this. Our sex powers have been given to us by our Higher Power. They are not to be used selfishly, but if we swing to the other extreme and regard those sex powers as disgusting or dirty, then we are as far off the beam as ever. The truth is that *we do not know what to do with those sex powers.* And – as with everything else in our lives – when we do not know what to do, we turn to our Higher Power in Steps 10 and 11, as the next paragraph tells us.

Whatever our ideal turns out to be, we must be willing to grow toward it. We must be willing to make amends where we have done harm, provided that we do not bring about still more harm in so doing. In other words, we treat sex as we would any other problem. In meditation, we ask God what we should do about each specific matter. The right answer will come, if we want it.

It's all very well to have an ideal, an ideal which has come to us through our relationship with our Higher Power. But how are we going to try to achieve that ideal?

The answer is pretty simple. We didn't come up with the ideal to begin with: we were taught it by our Higher Power, through our practice of Steps 10 and 11. So working towards that ideal will also have to be done with the help of our Higher Power. We can't change our own behavior – if we could, we wouldn't need to practice this Program at all. As we grow towards our ideal, therefore, we let ourselves be guided by whatever Higher Power we may choose.

As the Big Book says, "we treat sex and relationships as we would any other problem." We make amends, if doing so doesn't cause us more trouble (and the matter of amends in P-68 is not simple). But above all else we ask our Higher Power what we should do and for the strength to do it, and we can be sure that the right answer will come.

If this is so – if our sex and relationship problems are to be to dealt with in the same way as any other problem – then why do so many recovering alcoholics and addicts have continuing difficulties in this area? Well, one reason may be that *most recovering alcoholics and addicts don't deal with other problems by taking them to their Higher Power in Steps 10 and 11.* Most recovering alcoholics and addicts try to handle their own problems. They tend to think, "I recovered from alcoholism or addiction by handing it over to God and surrendering it completely. That's quite enough surrendering for one lifetime. Now I'm going to live the rest of my life my way."

That's why sex and relationship problems are such a problem in 12-Step fellowships. Our respective programs are full of people who've never troubled to hand over their will and lives to the care of God as they understand God, which is what Step 3 suggests. The only thing they've handed over to God is their core addiction. So when the Big Book suggests, as it does here, that "we treat sex and relationships as we would any other problem," if it turns out that we try to handle all our problems ourselves instead of using Steps 10 and 11, then we'll try to handle our sex and relationship problems ourselves too. The results of that tend to be disastrous – and sometimes tragic or fatal.

God alone can judge our sex situation. Counsel with persons is often desirable, but we let God be the final judge. We realize that some people are as fanatical about sex as others are loose. We avoid hysterical thinking or advice.

The Big Book makes it clear that solutions to our sex and relationship issues arise out of our relationship with our Higher Power. We may discuss our situation with others in Program, but if we let ourselves or other people be the judge of what we should do then we're headed for trouble.

If this is true, then the developing of a close, continuing relationship with our Higher Power has to be a top priority. That is another reason for the constant working of Steps 10 and 11. We can't depend on ourselves and we can't depend on other people. In the final analysis, all our answers must come from our Higher Power. That's not likely to happen if we spend most of our lives listening to what's going in in our heads or to the advice of other people. Time spent in the practice of Steps 10 and 11 is always a valuable investment. It enables us to deepen the only relationship that can truly help us in this or any other matter.

People tend to be fanatical about sex. That's easy for us to understand, because we used to be fanatics ourselves. A significant part of recovery is learning to let other people be fanatics. We're better off when we avoid hysterical people and hysterical thinking. We're better off when we seek counsel with other people instead of advice from them.

Suppose we fall short of the chosen ideal and stumble? Does this mean we are going to get drunk? Some people tell us so. But this is only a half-truth. It depends on us and on our motives. If we are sorry for what we have done, and have the honest desire to let God take us to better things, we believe we will be forgiven and will have learned our lesson. If we are not sorry, and our conduct continues to harm others, we are quite sure to drink. We are not theorizing. These are facts out of our experience.

Here is the great difference between recovery from sex and relationship addiction on the one hand, and recovery from alcoholism, drug addiction, and other "hard" addictions on the other.

Complete abstinence from alcohol or drugs is not merely achievable for alcoholics and addicts: it's mandatory for recovery. Eventually, as the Big Book promises, they reach a position of neutrality with respect to drugs and alcohol. They have not "sworn off" – instead, says the Big Book, the problem has been removed.

That will probably never happen with our sex and relationship addiction. We may be able to live without alcohol and drugs, but unless we are leading a very isolated existence we will always encounter sex and relationship issues. We're meant to: as these pages of the Big Book suggest, our ability to engage in sex and have relationships is God-given. So the ideal that we develop for our future relationships, an ideal that we develop in fellowship with our Higher Power, always remains an ideal. Sometimes we are able to achieve it: sometimes we may fail.

But failure to meet the ideal we have set for ourselves is not the same as "slipping" with respect to alcohol or drugs. It's very different. When we don't attain our ideal, it's always because of selfishness, and we'll always be selfish to some extent, no matter how our behavior may have improved.

So when we fail, we do Step 10 all over again. Where were we selfish? Are we sorry for what we did? Are we convinced once more that our Higher Power needs to be running the show, not us? If we are, then we have learned an important lesson.

But if we don't view our situation in this way; if we think we were justified in what we did; if we think that we can somehow imitate ordinary people's behavior with respect to sex and relationships; if we think that we can pretty much do as we please; and if we continue to harm other people because of that behavior, then if we are also recovering alcoholics and addicts **we are sure to drink or drug again.** Sooner or later, our behavior will catch up with us.

You may want to see how many times the Big Book says that we may drink again. Perhaps you will be surprised how rarely it does this. But – as far as sex and relationships are concerned – the Big Book is uncompromising. If we go back to our old ways in this area of our lives, then we are certain to encounter serious problems.

Many recovering people in AA may disagree with this. They are directing their own lives when it comes to sex and relationships, and they feel they're doing a pretty good job. We have said elsewhere that we do not choose to be the arbiter of anyone's sex conduct, but even so you may want to think very hard about what these people are doing. Is such behavior with respect to sex and relationships based to some extent on selfishness and dishonesty? Is that the sort of behavior we committed to at the start of our recovery? And how long can we live that way before there is trouble? Do *you* want to live that sort of life? Do *you* want to find out for yourself if *you* can stay sober living like that? Or do you prefer to follow the recommendations of the Big Book, and leave the experimenting to other, supposedly recovering, members? As a wise person in AA once said, "The great advantage of long-term recovery is that it allows other people to go back out and make your mistakes for you."

To sum up about sex: We earnestly pray for the right ideal, for guidance in each questionable situation, for sanity, and for the strength to do the right thing. If sex is very troublesome, we throw ourselves the harder into helping others. We think of their needs and work for them. This takes us out of ourselves. It quiets the imperious urge, when to yield would mean heartache.

Here is a summary of what the Big Book has to say about sex and relationships.

We ask our Higher Power for our ideal when it comes to sex and relationships. We don't try and dream it up ourselves: we look to God as we understand God, through prayer and meditation, to provide that ideal for us.

We ask for guidance when things get difficult. If we talk to others, we talk to people with whom we can have a discussion, people who are long on listening and short on giving advice. We accept that we are not supposed to know automatically what we should do: that's what Step 10 is there for, to remind us that *we do not know what to do.* Instead, in Step 11 we ask our Higher Power in prayer and meditation for guidance, for sanity in sex and relationships, and for strength to work towards our ideal.

Sometimes sex and relationships can become troublesome. This can happen no matter how long we have been practicing what these few paragraphs recommend. Then Step 12 comes into its own. After all, the purpose of the practice of Steps 10 and 11, indeed the purpose of our entire recovery, has very little to do with us. It has to do with "fit[ting] ourselves to be of maximum use to God and the people about us." In Step 10, "we resolutely turn our thoughts to someone we can help." In Step 11, we gain the power to help them. In Step 12, we actually *do* help them. It's that usefulness to others, and not the attaining of a satisfactory sexual or intimate relationship, that is the true focus of recovery.

Some Stories of Recovery
from Sex and Relationship Addiction

What it was like, what happened, and what it is like now

1.

When I quit drinking a number of years ago, I knew I had a problem with pornography as well, and made a decision to stop using it at the same time I quit drinking. I did not go to AA immediately; I went to buy an AA Big Book two days after I quit drinking. Finding it was not available at my book store, I found several Adult Children of Alcoholic (ACA) books there, and since my dad was an alcoholic, I bought one of these and identified with much that I read. A few months later, I joined a therapy group led by a woman familiar with ACA issues who was a recovering alcoholic herself. She was also very familiar with sex addiction and had done much personal work in that area. Within a few months, I started attending AA, and shortly after that got involved with assorted recovery workshops, support groups, peer counseling, and so forth. I pretty much threw myself into recovery and found much relief.

I found that not acting out sexually in recovery was more difficult than not drinking. I find this is fairly common. I did not find it terribly difficult the first two years in recovery not to act out sexually, but I found myself talking about these issues more and more often in group. The therapist recommended that I consider going into in-patient treatment for sexual addiction. I would also be able to work on family-of-origin issues there. I was reluctant at first, but with her encouragement and the encouragement of my AA sponsor who was in the group, I decided to go. It was hard leaving home to travel out of state to this facility. I was 35 at the time. It was a difficult but rewarding experience, and I have fond memories of the time there and the people I met. I was there for 30 days; the last week of treatment my wife came and attended some counseling sessions and group activities with me.

We were asked to commit to a three-month period of celibacy when treatment started. I knew this would be difficult, but I was committed to my recovery and to doing all I could to living a more healthy lifestyle. I made it through the treatment period without acting out. At times this was very difficult, but the group support and the immersion in all the activities helped considerably. I recall leaving the treatment facility on a Saturday afternoon. Our return flight back home wasn't until Sunday morning. My mother and 14 month-old son had made the trip to the treatment center with my wife, and we all spent the night together in a motel room before the return trip the next day. I remember how good it felt to be close to my wife that night in bed; I still recall it to this day. Her body was warm and soft and even though we refrained from any serious physical contact, it just felt good to be near her. Refraining from sex was not easy. I think it made me more aware of my real relationship with my wife and who she was as a person. On the flight back home the next morning I remember enjoying simply talking with my wife. It reminded me of when I first met her and we started dating; I felt that same energy and attraction to her. I think with sexual considerations out of the way it opened me up again to seeing my wife as a person whom I cared about and was trying to get to know again.

I started attending SLAA meetings not long after I got back home. I attended the therapy group weekly and talked with my sponsor regularly during this time as well as attending AA meetings. All this support was extremely valuable. My wife also was very supportive. My wife is an attractive woman but I focused on her weight a great deal back then and I "knew" I would be much happier if she was a "little" thinner: our sex life be exciting and wonderful. This caused problems in our marriage because the message I was sending was that I was not happy with my wife as she was. I'm clear now that, even if she were at some supposed "ideal weight,", I would have probably focused on some other physical attribute or behavior or hers that "needed changing" for me to be happy. I think this is part of the problem for many of us: this objectifying of our partner, our need for them to be a certain way and to act a certain way for us to be happy. I had a lot to learn about true intimacy which, quite frankly, was scary to me. So much of what I considered intimacy only involved sexual passion.

Looking back, all the support I had during this withdrawal period helped me immensely to get through it. Talking about my feelings about this in the therapy group and with recovery friends was a huge help. What I realized in my life through this period was that I had to "be" with sexual feelings without acting on them - so I got to experience that. What came up was loneliness and neediness and vulnerability, even feelings of shame and not feeling good about myself at all. I saw that at times I made my wife into a "goddess" who could save me from all this. I had attached so much value to sex that really wasn't about sex at all. I'm convinced that a withdrawal period is absolutely necessary to begin recovery from this obsession. I got to experience what it is to be truly human during this time. Some of the feelings were very painful, but they passed, and I have to say that I also got to experience joy and happiness in ways that I had not often felt. I know also that I developed strength of character and confidence by going through this process. We discover that things we think we can't do are achievable with the help of our Higher Power. There were a few occasions during this celibacy period that my wife and would flirt and play around. I can recall being very emotionally and sexually stimulated by this; it nearly led to the breaking of my celibacy during this period, but I am glad that we were able to abstain. Of course, having sex with my wife wouldn't have been the worst thing in the world, even at that time, but I did find a much closer connection to her in the long run by honoring my commitment. I was able to experience healthy feelings of desire and playfulness, I had to deal with my wife as a person, and I got to know her and myself much better. I saw that I could live and prosper without being sexual. I have to say that my relationship with my wife, and our sex life, improved substantially after this withdrawal period. That was surely one of the gifts I got from this experience. I saw that I could survive so many of the painful emotional feelings that came up during this period without resorting to acting out sexually to fix them, and I'm grateful for that.

And so to the present. Even though I stayed sober and active in 12-Step programs and continue with other spiritual practices, abstaining from acting out sexually became increasingly difficult. I remained married and relatively happy, but I still struggled in this area. I was no longer going to meetings which dealt with my sexual addiction. A close friend was involved in the P-68 group: I was intrigued with their approach to the problem of sex and relationship addiction, which is to follow the suggestions of the AA Big Book, create an abstinence list, and work closely with someone in the group. The acting out I had been doing with pornography was briefer and in some ways "lighter" than years ago, but I still found that I could not leave it alone. What happened after these escapades was always the same for me. I felt awful and would resolve not to do it again, but I'd find myself acting out to some extent weeks or months later. As so often happens, after a period of "being good," somehow I felt entitled to indulge in some acting out. The first time doing this would generally be exciting and stimulating, but then I couldn't stop. It always ended the same way, in guilty and shameful feelings about myself, together with a commitment to do "better". I knew, though, at a deeper level that unless something changed with me this was a forlorn hope.

After the last episode, I called my friend in P-68 and put together an abstinence list. He told me I could change anything on the list I wanted; all I had to do was call him first. This seemed to take a weight off my back. It felt like freedom reined in by common sense, collaboration, and responsibility. I had been actively working Steps 10, 11, and 12 for the last several years, but I had not wholeheartedly committed to turning my sexual addiction over to my Higher Power and truly relying on that Power for guidance. I came to realize that I have this in common with a lot of people who have long-term recovery from other addictions. I felt immediate relief that Sunday morning, when I put together the abstinence list and went over this with my friend on the telephone. We met a few days later, tweaked the list a little, and had a good discussion about this process. I have met regularly with him during this "second" period in my life of abstinence and I find these meetings helpful. Support from meetings and from other friends committed to this process have also been necessary for me.

This period of abstinence is different in many ways from the previous one. As I have grown older, and maybe grown spiritually too, abstinence seems a bit easier. Additionally, I was "sick and tired of being sick and tired," and now I know there is a solution. I didn't want to spend the rest of my life living in the bondage of sexual addiction. And – just as with alcohol - this addiction only gets worse, not better. I had had fears of being in my 60's, glued to my computer on weekday mornings, acting out sexually while my wife was at work; and I do not want to live that way. I have felt a great sense of freedom and of closeness to my Higher Power and more peace of mind since I recommitted myself a few months ago. Again, I find sex with my wife more enjoyable and stimulating now.

As the months pass, I still at certain times feel the temptation to act out "lightly." It's the old thought that, since I have abstained for a number of months from this activity, I am entitled to some "time off." Of course, that will lead to the same place I started: shame and despair, feeling bad about myself, and telling myself that I have got to stop.

Abstinence can never been done perfectly; slips, however they are defined, may happen more often in recovery from sexual addiction than from abstinence from alcohol; but with the help of God as I understand God, and members of P-68, I find that I have resources now to stay the course. It is good to know that, as I gain time in this practice, my Higher Power is leading me to a reasonable, sane and happy sex life – a sane and sensible life in general.

2.

I did not realize the experience I was having because it was familiar. I had been "between" relationships before but soon resolved the problem with new relationships. My experience of withdrawal was characterized by fear, depression, agitation and suicidal ideation. My experience I believe was further complicated by the fact that it occurred around the holidays, which has always been an emotional time for me.

It has been my experience that, for men, withdrawal is "solved" by going to a bar, by pornography, a dating website, a prostitute; or by other addictions like food, alcohol, drugs etc. It felt like an impending disaster with no end.

Further, having an abstinence list and realizing that sex was not an option to solve the terrible problem made the experience seem like a horrible trap. I hated to see night and I hated to see day. This is not a matter that can be discussed with just anyone: in fact, it seems that only those who are in some sort of sex and relationship addiction program understand withdrawal. People in the other 12-Step programs seem to see no problem with sexual acting out, masturbation, etc., as long as you don't "use."

While going through withdrawal, I noticed a tendency to overeat, to watch too much television, and to think about past sexual relationships. I continued to feel an extreme longing for contact with another human being, particularly of course for the attention of a woman. On the other hand, it seemed to me that my emergence from withdrawal was coming quickly as I worked Steps 8 and 9, and in realizing the harm I caused others and myself through relationships. I begin to realize the toxic way I used and abused others in relationships, and I also came to see that another relationship was not the answer. I was not yet ready, and I am still not ready. Even now it is so difficult for me to accept that a woman is not the answer to all of my problems.

I have sought to have compassion, concern and forgiveness toward others. I have sought through prayer and meditation to watch my mind and begin to find love and God on the inside, not the outside. My challenge today is to avoid dwelling on "dating plans" and basing my future on how to "do the relationship thing right." For me, thinking in this way is like an alcoholic fantasizing about drinking normally.

3.

I suppose my story only seems different because it happened to me, but I suspect that many can relate to my experiences. I have always seemed to manage to be in a relationship, but I had never given any thought to the link between each relationship and why I kept going back out. I have known all my life that I was co-dependent, but I always regarded it as something that was a necessity to being a man. I felt as if I needed a lover to be whole. As far back as I can remember I have had a girlfriend or a "special friend" and that made me amount to something (or so I believed). I hopped from relationship to relationship, never seeming able to get my fill. I never seemed to look back to see if I had hurt anyone because I was focused on who would be my next companion. Sex itself was not too important until I became a heavy drug and alcohol user in my late teens. It was hard for me to get close to anyone without thinking about running away as fast as I could. I always acted on that impulse. It seemed at the time to be my only option. I was addicted to relationships!

When I was 18 I started dating a woman that seemed to be everything I ever wanted. I thought I was in love – and then came the using and drinking. The relationship went from bad to worse. There was sex, but only out of drug- or alcohol-fueled emotions. I was looking for something that I could not quite put my finger on: something meaningful, not this feeling of dislike and discomfort towards someone that I supposedly loved. Drugs and alcohol kept me loyal for almost three years and then we parted to go to treatment. I came to Texas while she remained in Maryland. We pledged our commitment over the phone once we completed treatment and I thought about how badly I wanted to be in her arms. It didn't work out, of course.

Subsequent relationships were short-lived, always ending with me running away once again. I was engulfed with friends, booze, casual meaningless encounters, and drugs. I ran in circles and hurt as many partners as I could, and I even went back to some of them and repeated my wrongdoings. After reuniting with a past woman that I had "sworn off," I began to understand what I was doing to myself and everyone I came into contact with. It ended, of course, but I had learned something important.

It was not easy to let go. I had a difficult time, and still do on some days when I feel alone. I yearned for that woman's presence even though I knew it would hurt me physically and emotionally. The pain seemed endless.

I was introduced to a new way of life that not only gave me direction, but invited me to join with several others who knew exactly what I felt. As the pain went away, I began to feel okay with myself. I learned how to make friends instead of looking for lovers that I knew I would lie to.

Most of all I discovered what it is to respect myself and therefore respect others.

4.

My withdrawal experience was one of the toughest, most painful experiences in my life. I went from having a girlfriend of five years, going to massage parlors regularly when out of town, sleeping regularly with two girlfriends that I had out of town, flirting and messing around with women whenever I could, to … nothing.

My old way of life had worked pretty well for a good period of time until my girlfriend found out about some of the infidelity, and then the fun stopped. My shame and guilt were overwhelming.

There were several reasons I agreed to stop everything and to work for recovery in this area of my life. First, I saw how it miraculously worked with a good friend of mine, and how it transformed his life. Second, I already understood from my alcoholism that recovery meant abstinence. And finally, I was hopeless and desperate.

I was told that the process of withdrawal would take a long time. It would be to my benefit if I were to be celibate for the period during which I was working my Steps in this program. A significant part of my recovery was my abstinence list, in which I wrote down guidelines for my behavior and activities that I believed I could abstain from with the help of my Higher Power). I could add to, or delete items from this list whenever I wished, as long as I let my sponsor know before I acted on them. This would keep me accountable for my actions.

This period of abstinence has allowed me to work the Steps with more focus and clarity. I believe it has helped in renewing my relationship with myself and my Higher Power, and given me an understanding of an ideal for sex and relationships, and the characteristics that I wish my partner to possess.

5.

My withdrawal experience has been the most difficult experience of my life.

It lasted about four or five months. I had relapsed into alcoholism and addiction once again and been out for about five days. Before that, I had had about six months of sobriety. However, during that time I had jumped from relationship to relationship without any breaks in between.

I had been in AA for over ten years and would work the Steps to the best of my ability. I would get a period of sobriety and then jump into a relationship as soon as I started feeling better from my previous relapse. I never chose women that were good for me – not that I was an upstanding gentleman myself, of course. I tended to attract women who were like me, because my behavior was still sick. When the relationship blew up and we had a big falling out, I would immediately look for something to fill that void: attention, one night stands, pornography, or even just the company of a "friend" - always female, though. I used women as a drug to make me feel better because I didn't feel good about myself. I have always felt insecure and full of fear, but I acted as if I was confident and had it together. I was driven by vanity, by the kind of car I had, by the job I had, and by my physical appearance, and in just the same way the women I dated had to look great on the outside. I constantly bragged to make myself seem better than I really was, so I could get validation from others. People would think I was cocky and arrogant, but the truth is that if anyone had known what was going on in my head, they would see I was just a scared boy trying to be a man. My definition of a "man" was far from the reality: I was never taught that a real man is loving, caring, respectful, willing to help others, humble, and a protector. I rarely showed these qualities: I was what some might consider a predator.

My definition of sex had been warped since I was a child. I was raised in a strict religious family and my understanding of sex was very vague. I was only told that if I had it outside of marriage it was a sin, so I learned about sex at a young age through talking to the other boys at school and through pornography. No wonder I had a twisted view of sex.

When I finally hit bottom, I was still a young man in my late twenties. I was sober at the time, but my behavior during that period of sobriety had been selfish and dishonest. At the end of one of my relationships, I went out looking for sex, and met up with some friends at a night club. I realized I had the urge to drink, but the thought came, "Maybe you can relate to the women at this club better, maybe they will want you more if you're drinking with them."

So that's what I did. I was off on another five-day bender and almost checked myself into my eighth rehab. But this time I didn't end up in rehab. My sponsor let me stay with him, and I started working the Steps once again. This time, I got on my knees and asked God to help me. I was done: I decided I would do anything to stay sober. I was really tired of doing the same thing over and over. Even all the sex and everything that went with it had gotten old to me.

I discussed my Fifth Step with my sponsor, and after ten minutes of listening to it he said that it was the worst sex inventory he had ever heard and he didn't know if he could help me. I was embarrassed, but looking back I truly believe God was talking through him because it motivated me to get the help I needed.

On his advice, I approached a man who was a recovering sex and love addict and who went to the same AA meeting as I did. I told him my story and he chuckled at me, shook his head, sighed, and said, "Yes, I believe you've got what I have. Now what are you going to do?" We sat for a long time. We discussed what he called an abstinence list and we talked about withdrawal. I was a little nervous about abstaining from my old behavior because, in a way, my behavior was what defined who I was. But I was willing to do anything at this point. I wrote out some of the destructive behaviors that I couldn't stop and read them to him.

Now the key insight was that I was obviously powerless over these behaviors and couldn't stop doing them. However, with the help of God, and by sharing this list with my sponsor, I gave them over to God and started my painful journey. My withdrawal lasted around six months, but the last few months were not as difficult as the beginning.

I recommend to anyone doing this not to take the withdrawal process gradually, as an alcoholic might try to wean himself off drinking by switching to beer. Stopping each behavior quickly with the help of my Higher Power by placing it on my abstinence list was what worked. It's also worked for the few others I know in Program that have followed this same path.

That's the good news. The bad news is that it was quite easily the most painful experience I have ever gone through. I thought about it all day long: I felt very ugly on the inside and I probably didn't look too good on the outside. My mind was fixed on a recent ex-girlfriend and I couldn't seem to stop obsessing about her. This went on for months. It was a very different experience from coming off drugs or alcohol, where the withdrawal is over in a week or two. This seemed to last for ever. Previously, I constantly sought things on the outside to make me feel better, and when those things let me down I was devastated and realized I hated myself.

But this time it was different. I had turned to God because I was in so much pain. I prayed and asked Him to make me a whole man, a man who wanted only Him and His love. For the first time in my life, I was completely dependent upon God, and as a result I started to change. People around me started to notice it before I did.

Today I can say I am a whole man. I am in a happy relationship with a beautiful woman who would have never been interested in me before. I have a new attitude and outlook on sex and relationships. Because I worked the Steps and followed the suggestions of others in Program, I am no longer a fearful boy; I am now well on the way to becoming a whole man.

6.

Twelve years after stopping drinking and drugging, I finally gave up on my sex and relationship addiction.

The pattern of acting out on that addiction had been pretty much the same after I sobered up as it was before I sobered up. I would tend to be in a relationship with a woman for a long time, but there would always be women who were "friends" and with whom I would have secretive relationships – a sort of "reserve team," if you like, from whom I could pick someone when that main relationship failed. And, sooner or later, that main relationship always did fail. It used to puzzle me what was wrong with the women I had these long relationships with. Why did they always turn out to be no good? I never realized that the common factor in all those failed relationships was me.

The result of having these long-term relationships and the "reserve team" was that I was never by myself, never "between relationships." A long-term relationship had just ended when I awoke one Saturday morning thinking to myself, "I should really get in touch with S." Never mind that S. had told me some months previously that if she ever saw me again it would be too soon …. And – for some reason – the thought about calling S. was immediately followed by another thought … and that other thought was, "You can't keep living like this."

So instead of calling S., I called someone in AA that I knew was also a recovering sex and relationship addict. (In fact, I'd kept well away from him up to that point precisely because he *was* a sex and relationship addict.) With him, I went to my first meeting … and learned about withdrawal.

It seemed to me that I was probably one of those special people who could manage quite well without a period of withdrawal. So I put it off for some time. I also started to notice that there didn't seem to be much recovery in the meetings I was attending. Most men shared about how they had "acted out" during the previous week. If "recovery" simply meant "fessing up" about my sex and relationship-based life, I didn't think I was interested.

After three months, a small group of us went off by ourselves to explore what real recovery might mean. Reluctantly, I also began my own withdrawal. There's no point in talking about how withdrawal feels: it's simply awful, that's all. With the help of my little group, I made it through the period of five months or so. Shortly afterwards, I met another woman … and we are still together, eighteen years later.

Why is withdrawal so painful? I think it's because the issue of what woman was in my life dominated everything else that I thought, that I felt, that I did, that I was. The most fundamental question was always, "Where is the woman?" The answer to that question would determine everything else in my life – even what continent I lived on. (I have changed continents twice based solely on the answer to that question.) So if a man defines himself fundamentally in terms of a woman, then when he decides he will withdraw from any such relationship completely for a period of time he no longer knows who he is. And for five months, I no longer knew who I was, and learned to let my Higher Power determine that whole matter for me.

True recovery from sex and relationship addiction is hard. Recently, I have once more become involved with a small group of like-minded men who believe that our sex lives and our relationships must be placed in their entirety in the hands of a Higher Power. For me to try and control what happens there is simply to remain in the obsession with sex and relationships. I have come to see that who I may be with, what my relationship with that woman may be, even whether I am in a relationship at all, is simply none of my business. And I'm much happier when I stay out of stuff that's none of my business.

Appendix:
Original Meditation Suggestions

The earliest P-68 meetings used the following meditation exercises. These were subsequently changed because they do not appear in the AA Big Book, on which P-68 is closely based. They are printed here in the hope that some people may find them useful.

Step 10 "meditation"

1. Set a timer for five minutes. Say this (or something similar):
We are going to do five minutes of Step 10 meditation. I will start the timer, and then suggest to you what to do.

[Start the timer.]

Let's close or half-close our eyes and breathe normally.

On each in-breath, and on each out-breath, we are going to say a silent word to ourselves. The word is *Rising* on the in-breath, and *Falling* on the out-breath, as our stomach rises and falls. Breathe normally, and say *Rising* to yourself on the in-breath, and *Falling* on the out-breath.

[Let everyone do this for three or four breaths.]

After doing this for a while, your mind will start to wander. Perhaps you start thinking about something. Don't try and control your mind. Don't tell it what to do. Simply follow it, and say *Thinking, thinking* for just as long as it thinks.

Then perhaps you hear a noise, and start listening to it. For as long as your mind is listening, say *Listening, listening*. Don't try and control your mind. Just say a silent word on each in-breath and out-breath: *Thinking, thinking,* or *feeling, feeling*, or *listening, listening*.

After a while your mind will stop, because it doesn't like being watched. If that happens, go back to *Rising, falling.*

[Wait till the timer sounds.]

Step 11 "meditation"

We are going to do five minutes of Step 11 meditation. I will start the timer, and then suggest to you what to do.

[Start the timer.]

Let's close or half-close our eyes and breathe normally.

Watch the in-breath begin, continue, and end. Then watch the out-breath begin, continue, and end. Perhaps there is a pause after the out-breath. Then the next in-breath begins, continues, and ends, and the next out-breath begins, continues, and ends. Watch the in-breath all the way in. Watch the out-breath all the way out. If your mind wanders, gently bring it back to watch the in-breath all the way in, and the out-breath all the way out.

[Wait till the timer sounds.]